TUB FARMING

Grow Vegetables Anywhere in Containers

Mary Johnson

Garden Way Publishing
Charlotte, Vermont 05445

Designer: Leon Danilovics

Illustrator: Jim Steven

Printed in the United States

Library of Congress Cataloging in Publication Data

Johnson, Mary, 1952–
    Tub farming.

    1. Vegetable gardening. 2. Container gardening.
I. Title.
SB324.4.J64   635   78-11821
ISBN 0-88266-138-8 pbk.

Contents

Found in the Gardens of Babylon, along the Appian way, on the banks of the Seine, around countless English cottages and, finally, on California patios everywhere...container gardening cannot be claimed as an Orwellian discovery! But modern science and technology have contributed significantly to our ability to produce farm quality vegetables in a bushel basket on your front porch! Improved strains and varieties of all popular garden vegetation permit full-size fruitage with minimal root space. Advances in lightweight soil mixes provide effective draïnage with a disease-free growing medium. And, complete planting and growing systems offered by leading horticultural suppliers make Tub Farming an almost carefree experience. Of course, "secrets of the ages," the "wisdom of experience," and traditional folklore cannot be overlooked in the successful nurturing of a Tub Farm on your porch or in your living room!

1

Essentials

Proper light, water and
temperatures are essential to
any plant's survival. Farming
in a tub or other pot requires
that these and other needs are
met for good crops of all
vegetables, flowers and
fruits.

Indoors, these Better Boy hybrid tomato plants grew and produced tomatoes from January until December.

How does Tub Farming differ from outdoor gardening? Do I need to water my containers more often? Surely I can't grow watermelons on my balcony! I have a backyard and don't need to garden in pots—but should I, in order to save myself weeding and animal damage? Can I grow tomato and cucumber plants together in one tub?

With all the questions and misinformation that have evolved about container gardening, this concise illustrated how-to book will guide you through the maze of gardening techniques, enabling you to successfully grow plants anywhere without a garden.

The advantages of farming in tubs are even more numerous than conventional gardening in the ground:

- Enjoy luscious vine-ripened vegetables regardless of where you live.
- It is less work—containers are closer to a water source, grouped together, and located just outside your door.
- Ground space may not be available if you live in an apartment, townhouse, or mobile home.
- Almost any plant can be grown in a tub—vegetables, flowers, bushes, even fruit trees.
- Mobile containers allow you to follow the sun, avoiding shade from buildings or trees during the day.

Vegetables can be decorative as well as functional as this cabbage proves.

- Bring seasonal changes to your home by rotating plants in containers.

- The growing season can be extended by moving containers indoors during frost.

- Containers can be protected from rabbits, gophers, squirrels, birds and crawling insects.

- There are no long rows to hoe or weeds to hand-pull.

- Children can have their own mini-garden in a container which requires little upkeep or close attention.

- It's fun!

One doesn't have to be a food technologist to know that a vine-ripened fruit tastes and looks better than one that was picked green, bathed in ethylene gas to give it color, and sits still hard as a rock on your supermarket shelf.

Psychologists contend that having plants in our environment is vital to a healthy state of mind. In earlier times we were all closer to nature, attuned to its rhythm. Today we have to compensate for the lack of greenery, and container gardening gives everyone that opportunity, regardless of where each individual lives.

Decorating with tropical plants is essential to architects or designers. But indoor and outdoor vegetable decorating is still in its infancy. A coffee plant or ornamental cabbage is quite a conversation piece on a living room table. Tubs of sweet potato vines or pole beans near a window will shade a room during hot summer afternoons. Pots of herbs bring an outdoor look and smell to any windowless kitchen or bathroom.

Convenience, taste, fun, decoration, economy, a soothing atmosphere—all are good reasons to begin farming in tubs. We all would like to just drop seeds in the ground and without any effort from us, begin to crank out crops like a factory. But just like raising children, adopted plants need care and nurture to develop into healthy, mature individuals. This Tub Farming book is meant to be a guide to help you grow the most successful vegetables with the least amount of work. Only the most successful, convenient, time-saving techniques are presented. You can always think up more elaborate, complicated routines on your own without the help of a book. Give it a try—it's easy and your kids will no longer believe that carrots grow in plastic bags!

Light

Of the three major requirements for plant growth—light, temperature and moisture—light is usually the hardest to control. If your container garden is shaded or on the north side of your building, you probably won't move just to satisfy your plants' sunshine requirements.

Plants such as parsley, leaf lettuce, chives, radishes, and cabbage do fairly well with four hours of direct sunlight. All other vegetables need a minimum of 6 hours of direct light. Full sunlight on a clear day is about 10,000 foot candles. Most vegetables can use only 2,500-5,000 footcandles. Plant leaves just can't utilize light fast enough. So you do have a fudge factor, but the minute a cloud rolls across the sky, the intensity is cut down. If you live in a clear, smog-free area, you can

Light intensity reaching plants is decreased by shade trees, fog or smog; but increased by the reflection from light-colored walls.

plant your crops in an area which is partially shaded during the day. But in frequently cloudy or foggy areas, the plants may need 8-10 hours of direct light per day.

Always plant taller crops such as corn on the north side of containers with shorter crops. Keep all containers away from trees since the foliage will shade your garden during some part of the day. In limited spaces where little sunlight is reaching the plants, staple aluminum foil to plastic and hang panels on the east and west sides of your garden area. Train heat-loving plants and fruits such as eggplant and tomatoes against a light-colored wall to utilize the reflected light and heat.

Winter gardens that have received no supplemental artificial light should be positioned to receive full sun all day, such as a window facing south or southwest.

Temperature—Macroclimates

There are two considerations essential to good vegetable development. The first is frost tenderness, the second is the growing temperature preferred by the species.

Vegetables which are tolerant of some frost are: *beets, broccoli, Brussels sprouts, cabbage, onions, radishes, spinach.* Those intolerant of being frostbitten are: *carrots, cauliflower, endive, eggplant, lettuce, peas, peppers, Swiss chard, tomatoes.*

A last-average-frost-date-map is not included here because there are so many variables within a zone. Spring temperature will always be cooler if you are on a mountain top or in the valley, but a map will only give you the average. Check with your local weather service for spring and fall average frost dates.

The vegetables which are harvested for their leaves, tips, roots or stems are cool-season crops. Those which are grown for their fruit need warmer seasons.

Cool-season crops grow best in the spring or early fall when temperatures average 45-70°F. When hotter weather approaches, they act like the warm-season vegetables and begin producing seed and fruits. The trouble is that we want to interfere with nature's course and prohibit them from producing seed, since our human tastes have developed a preference for eating the foliage and roots of these plants. To interfere with nature's plan, we plant these species only during cooler weather and enjoy home-grown lettuce only in the spring and fall. Cool-season crops include: *beets, broccoli, Brussels sprouts, cabbage, carrots, cauliflower, endive, lettuce, onions, peas, radishes, spinach, and Swiss chard.*

Warm-season crops go through similar life cycles of growing foliage and roots in the spring, followed by seeds and fruits in the heat of summer. The only difference is that we humans have turned up our noses at eating tomato leaves or cucumber roots, and prefer instead to eat the fruits of these plants. In order to get a bigger harvest of these fruits, the warm-season species are not set outside before temperatures of 65-80°F are common. If they are planted outside too early,

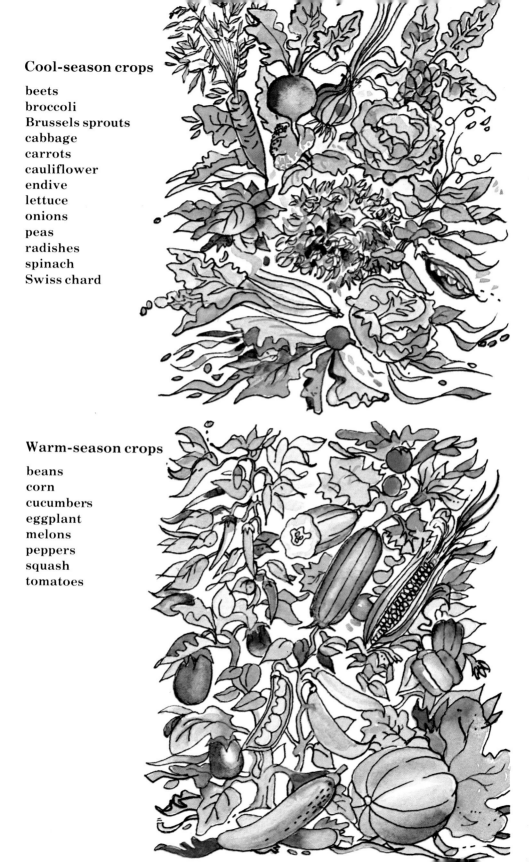

Cool-season crops

beets
broccoli
Brussels sprouts
cabbage
carrots
cauliflower
endive
lettuce
onions
peas
radishes
spinach
Swiss chard

Warm-season crops

beans
corn
cucumbers
eggplant
melons
peppers
squash
tomatoes

they may be damaged by frost, or will sit there and not have enough energy to grow. Warm-season crops include: *beans, corn, cucumbers, eggplant, melons, peppers, squash and tomatoes.*

If you try to grow cool-season crops in an air-conditioned room in the summer, you will still be foiled. Some plants such as radishes, lettuce and spinach will begin to flower when the day length becomes longer than 12 hours. These are called long-day plants. Others such as sweet potatoes, lima beans, June-bearing strawberries, chrysanthemums and poinsettias will flower only with short days and long nights. Hay fever sufferers can find relief in the far north since ragweed refuses to flower when sunlight shines for more than 14 hours. Day-neutral plants such as tomatoes, everbearing strawberries and peppers don't care how long the sun shines, and only then is temperature the deciding factor.

Besides cool- and warm-season crops, there are early and late varieties of vegetable species. An early variety will produce a crop with less total summer heat than a later maturing variety. An early variety may not mature in the number of days indicated in the most northern climates, but it will produce. Early vegetable varieties can be used as cool-season crops even in semi-tropical areas.

Microclimates

In any area, you can manipulate temperatures surrounding your containers. Farmers have to live with the elements the way they fall from the sky, but you can modify them very successfully.

Microclimates can be nurtured within your tubs. By setting plants close together, you not only utilize your space more efficiently, but the leaves will overlap and form an umbrella, almost a micro greenhouse climate. The air below is trapped, reducing the extreme changes from hot to cold in the morning and evening. Being

protected, the soil will not dry out as fast or form cracks caused by fast moisture loss.

If temperatures dip too low during the summer to ripen fruit, place containers against a south wall. If there still isn't enough heat reflected, hang aluminum foil or a mirror behind the pot.

If too much reflected heat is your problem, use a mulch to keep the roots cooler and moisten it often. Water the surface of your patio to increase humidity and move containers away from walls. Train ivy or other vines to cover bare walls to cut down on heat and light reflection.

Cities certainly get hotter than the countryside. Sun and heat bouncing off pavement is liable to cook your containerized plants. Shield them from this reflection by putting screens or bushes on the street side of your flowers and vegetables. Top floors of city high-rises are cooler because they are further removed from the reflected energy.

If fall frost and rains come too early for you, move your containers to a spot protected overhead, cover with a bag, or move the container indoors.

Water

For every pound of lettuce that you harvest from your containers, 400 pounds of water were used in its growth. Amazing? If you had to drink as much as a corn plant just to stay even with the water it was losing each day to the air, you would have to drink 10-15 gallons. That's 160-240 glasses of water every day.

Now it should be easy to realize why lack of water will cause radishes to become hard and woody, carrots stumpy, lettuce bitter and tomatoes to drop blossoms.

When a plant is not getting its full quota, it is under water stress. Some flowers seem to bloom more, but all vegetables suffer setbacks and never seem to recover.

How should you supply this vast amount of water to your plants? Containerized plants are exposed to drying air on all sides, even the bottom. This means the soil will dry out more quickly from the sun

Top: When plants are not watered deeply, shallow rooting and salt damage occurs. Bottom: Water evaporates more quickly from small or porous pots, therefore water these pots more frequently than others.

For every pound of leaves and raw vegetables from a plant, 400 pounds of water were used in its growth.

1 lb.

and wind than plants in the ground. Plants in small containers are more susceptible to quick drying.

Always use lukewarm water. It takes somewhere between 4-6 hours for the soil to regain the heat lost to the cold water. The plant roots try to readjust instead of using their energy for their primary functions of growth.

Check the soil daily. Most containers will need a deep watering every morning, and in hot weather more often. Late afternoon watering invites trouble from plant diseases. If you must water in the evening, use a drip irrigation system and avoid wetting the leaves. Too many gardeners are inclined to wet the soil surface without allowing deep water penetration. This not only wastes water, but encourages surface rooting which makes plants even more susceptible to drought.

Water thoroughly enough so that water reaches the bottom of the pot and drains through. Here are two good ways of telling whether or not the soil needs moisture. Check the top inch of soil. If your finger feels dry, then water. Or press a piece of newspaper on the surface. If it instantly becomes damp, there is no need yet to water.

Water as a direct jet on the surface can damage the soil structure and expose the roots. Use a watering can or fine mist adjustment on a hose.

There are several systems for vacation watering. If pots are grouped together and set on a moist gravel bed, humidity is increased

and less drying results. To simplify this same process, bury pots to their rims in a large box of moist sand (or peat moss) in a shady location. If you don't mind sharing your bathtub, run 2-3 inches of water into the tub and set the pots in the water. Nylon or cord wicks forced into the soil through the drainage holes will absorb water from a pan or sink filled with water. The best system is to ask a friend to tend your plants if you will be gone more than a couple of days.

Containers

The primary function of a container is holding the plant and its root system together. Clay pots, plastic pots, milk cartons, gutter pipe, tires, cement blocks, wash tubs, redwood troughs, plastic bags, whiskey barrels, bleach bottles, a plastic bag of potting soil poked with a few

drainage holes, virtually anything with connected sides will serve as a plant garden.

Following are some guidelines on how to choose the container that will be most pleasing to you while it serves its primary function.

The deeper the soil, the less often it will need watering. But do not pot into containers that are larger than the roots of your plants demand. The soil remains wet and encourages rot and other problems. A container that is too small will prevent root crops from maturing and force other roots to grow around the soil ball. Plants which are root bound are unable to effectively transport nutrients, water, and gases to the above-ground plant parts. For trees or tall house plants, the container should be 1/3 to 1/2 the height of the plant.

All containers should have drainage holes. If yours do not, and you are unwilling to drill holes in them, layer pebbles or broken crockery several inches deep in the bottom of the container. This allows all the soil to drain instead of remaining a soggy invitation to

Nearly anything can be used as a container. The honeycomb of this wasp's nest was set in a pot, filled with soil, then positioned inside the outer shell.

disease or suffocating rootlets. Porous containers such as clay, fiber or wooden pots dry out much faster than plastic, metal or waxy ones. Porous containers need to be watered twice as often just to counteract evaporation loss.

A darker colored container absorbs more heat than a light color. This will get seedlings off to a faster start. But these containers may need more frequent watering and protection on extremely hot days. If you live in a hot, dry climate, use light-colored pots or shade the containers to prevent the roots of your plants from frying in the noon-day sun.

A good rule for moving containers is to do it before watering. A freshly watered 18-inch tub with garden soil can weigh 200 pounds. If your container is not mounted on wheels, a wide shovel wedged under the tub will slide well. Three or four sticks or rods helped the Egyptians roll stones to build the pyramids, and it will work for your container, too, without thousands of slaves to push. A burlap bag or rug will also work well as a skid to cradle the pot and pull it a short distance.

Soil

Just as there is no magical "right container," there is no "right soil." Anything will work—garden soil, sand, water, perlite, peat moss, and you have seen at least one plant somewhere growing out of a stone. Soil itself is not a necessary requirement for plant growth. How can this be after hearing so much about the correct mixture of items to make a good potting soil? The function of soil is not to be a deep, rich brown color. It is to support the plant, and provide a medium in which the roots can absorb moisture, nutrients and gas through the roots without suffocating.

Some container gardeners go out and dig up a spadeful of garden earth. This will only buy you trouble with dormant weed seeds, hibernating insects, soil-borne diseases, heaviness, compaction, and

Examples of good soil mixes for container gardening:
Top left: peat moss
Top right:Vegi-mix™
Bottom left: perlite
Bottom right: Jiffy Mix®

chemicals or salts that have run into the ground through rain water—not to mention the broken sewer-pipe leakage you had last year.

The container gardener has a distinct advantage over outdoor gardeners because he selects a soil that provides the essentials to the plant that makes it easy for himself while maximizing the plant's growth. This is why there are so many natural and artificial soil mixes—some are easier and more efficatious than others. Rather than giving you the gamut of possibilities, why not use the best, least-fuss soil mix? After all, why work harder for less productive soil?

The best thing to do is use an "artificial" soil mix called a peat-lite mix. Store brand names for these soils are Jiffy-Mix ®, Vegi-Mix, ™ etc. Everything contained in peat-lite and potting soil mixes is natural, they are just put together in amounts different than you would find naturally in the ground, then packaged in a plastic bag. The most common mixture is 1/2 perlite or vermiculite and 1/2 peat moss, with essential plant food and trace elements added.

Peat-lite mixes were developed to be lightweight—only half the weight of garden soil, even when wet. This is welcome news to container gardeners with weak porches or windowsills—and backs!

Seedlings such as beans (left) have a hard time pulling their seeds and shoots through crusted, rocky soil. Corn (right) can withstand poorer soil conditions since its seed is left underground.

Perlite or vermiculite in the mixture provides air spaces. These help drain away excess water instead of compacting, while providing air pockets so that the roots can "breathe." On the soil surface a garden soil can crust over, preventing water penetration. Peat-lite mixes do not crust over, allowing the water and oxygen to reach deep roots quickly.

Most commercial soil mixes have nutrients added which provide plants all their necessary food. These mixes or natural soils are never "used up." The nutrients do leach out with the run-off water and need to be replaced with plant food. But you need not "shift soil" every few years in your containers. How long has it been since the earth's soil has been replaced with all new fresh soil?

Even if you live on a farm, think of all the extra time you will have if you grow your garden in weed-free soil in containers—and certainly you will have fewer backaches from hoeing and pulling weeds!

If you are using garden soil and need to change the pH (acidity) outside the 6.0-7.5 range, which is ideal for most plants, contact your county agricultural agent for recommendations for adding lime, sulphur or peat moss.

After filling your container with soil, soak with enough water until some water seeps through the bottom drainage holes. In a container without holes, push your finger or a stick to the bottom of the tub to tell whether the water reached the bottom soil. Do not plant seeds or transplants before the soil has been saturated.

Seeds

All seeds are embryonic plants. They are alive and breathing, waiting for the right external conditions so that they can germinate, or break through their seed coat. Some seeds will keep less than five years before they use up their reserve food. By storing seeds in a tightly closed jar in a cool place, food is used less rapidly. For better germination, buy new seed annually. A seed's waterproof coating surrounds a growing point and two folded leaves that act as a food reserve. In some plants such as beans these leaves are pulled up through the soil with the growing point. A plant like corn sends the shoot up alone and uses the food below the soil. These cotyledon leaves that emerge with the shoot of most vegetable plants cannot fight hard crusted soil or they will never be able to pull themselves through a hardpan layer. After another set of true leaves unfolds above the cotyledons the seedling should be transplanted.

Now that you know how a plant starts life, which seeds should you use and why? Hybrid varieties are selections of plants that show

Standard seed produces large plants with full-sized vegetables (left); container varieties (center) bear full-sized vegetables on compact plants; midget varieties (right) produce tiny plants and vegetables.

desirable characteristics. These are mates between two varieties that give us plants with more uniformity, vigor, disease resistance, flavor, yield, earliness or other desirable qualities. Like mules of the animal kingdom, the cross between a jackass and mare produces an offspring stronger than either parent, but unable to have offspring itself. Similarly, seed from hybrid plant varieties cannot be saved to give you the same plant the next year. You must use new hybrid seed every time you plant.

Plant breeders have taken familiar vegetables, fruits and flowers and developed strains with full-sized flowers or vegetables which

spread only 3-5 feet maximum size. These varieties are little factories, being better photosynthesizers (growth producers) than other plants the same size or larger. These varieties are a must for container gardeners, since more crops can be grown in a very small space.

Besides seed that comes in packets, pelleted seed coated in layers of nutrient fertilizer and inert material as well as seed tape is available. These new ways to use seed make handling and planting much easier. Speed up the sprouting of hard-coated or slow-to-germinate parsley, peas, beans and corn by soaking in water for one day prior to planting. This will soften the seed coat and shorten sprouting time.

Plant seed or transplants and water well.
Place container in a plastic bag to retain moisture.
When seed sprouts or cutting roots, move to a sunny location.

Starting seeds indoors and later transplanting gives you an earlier start on the season, especially for long-season, late-maturing vegetables. Some plants do not like to have their roots disturbed, so plant in individual peat pots that can be set directly into the larger container. These fussy species include the vine crops—melons, cucumbers, squash as well as eggplant. All other seeds can be started in flats, peat pots, peat pellets, fiber cubes, boxes or other available containers and later transplanted, or sown directly in permanent containers.

Indoors or out, plant seed at a depth of 3-4 times the diameter of the seed. Seeds planted too deep may not reach the soil surface. There is no magic reason for planting in rows. The reason it is done in an outdoor garden is to distinguish easily the seedlings from the weeds and insure a safe walkway between seedlings.

Firm the soil over the seed so that it won't dry out before sprouting. If you are planting outdoors, be sure the soil is 65-70°F for warm-season crops or rotting of the seed will occur before rooting. Place a plastic food wrap or baggie over the soil after sowing to retain moisture and heat. Take it off as soon as growth is seen. Seeds need a soil temperature— not air temperature—of 70-80°F in order to germinate. If your containers are small and shallow, place them on a radiator or refrigerator top that gives off heat. For outdoor containers, place in a warm protected spot.

As soon as the shoots emerge above the soil, move to a well-lit area so that photosynthesis—the plant's food production—can begin.

Transplants

It may be more practical for you to buy seedlings from a nursery for your container garden. Both nursery seedlings or transplants you have grown from seed need the same care when they are transferred outside.

For about two weeks before you intend to plant, get them used to outdoor conditions. This is called hardening off. Set seedlings outside when the weather is sunny and frost is not expected. Exposing them to lower temperatures than the ones they're used to indoors will let them take that shock before transplanting. If you rush them through both adjustments at the same time, they may give up and die. Purplish-bronze foliage on cabbage, broccoli or cauliflower indicates they have been properly hardened off.

Avoid buying tall, lanky plants. They have too much foliage in proportion to their roots, and will suffer severe setbacks after transplanting.

Wait until early evening to transplant. The heat of the day may cause plants to wilt, never to recover. Dig a hole for each plant, water and let the moisture soak in. Only lift as many plants as you can handle in a few minutes, trying to preserve as much of the root ball as possible. Set the plant into the hole at its original depth. Planting too deep or shallow may stop growth. The only exception to this is tomatoes. Bury the stem including some true leaves. If the plant is taller than 6 inches, tip the rootball sideways so that it will not be planted too deeply. Transplants should go into the soil with as little disturbance as possible. After firming the rootball into the soil, water each plant thoroughly. Do not wait until all the transplants are in place before watering. Water daily for a week.

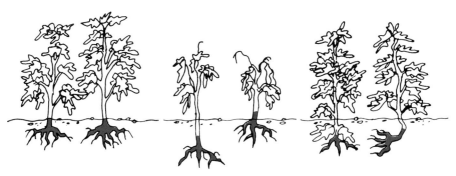

Correct depth   **Too deep,**   **The only exception:**
                     too shallow   **tomatoes. Bury**
                                        6 inches of stem.

Spacing

Ideally, what you want is to have plants spaced so that when mature, the plant leaves will touch each other, forming an umbrella which moderates the air temperature below, keeps the soil surface moist and utilizes space most efficiently. The best way to plan eventual spacing for your vegetable varieties is to read the recommendation on the seed pack or plant tag. Each variety is different and container or midget varieties of the same vegetable are radically different from standard varieties. If you sowed more seeds than you have room for, thin or pluck them out when the foliage of seedlings is touching.

Remember that planting in rows isn't necessary in weed-free containers that need no walking pathways.

For crops such as cucumbers, squashes or corn; seed packets recommend planting in "hills." These hills are not mounds of soil. The term means the practice of planting 5-6 seeds together. These should later be thinned to the 2-3 healthiest seedlings. These named varieties are especially suited to growing in containers. In a 6-inch pot or a 21-inch tub you can grow one of the following groups:

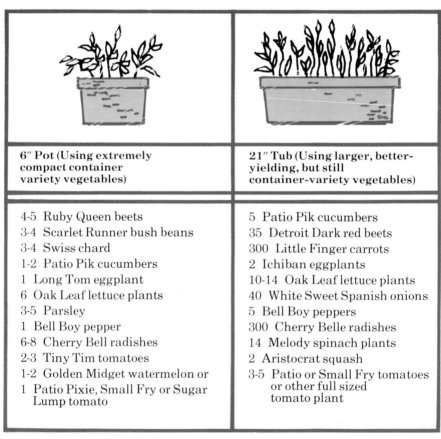

6″ Pot (Using extremely compact container variety vegetables)	21″ Tub (Using larger, better-yielding, but still container-variety vegetables)
4-5 Ruby Queen beets	5 Patio Pik cucumbers
3-4 Scarlet Runner bush beans	35 Detroit Dark red beets
3-4 Swiss chard	300 Little Finger carrots
1-2 Patio Pik cucumbers	2 Ichiban eggplants
1 Long Tom eggplant	10-14 Oak Leaf lettuce plants
6 Oak Leaf lettuce plants	40 White Sweet Spanish onions
3-5 Parsley	5 Bell Boy peppers
1 Bell Boy pepper	300 Cherry Belle radishes
6-8 Cherry Bell radishes	14 Melody spinach plants
2-3 Tiny Tim tomatoes	2 Aristocrat squash
1-2 Golden Midget watermelon or	3-5 Patio or Small Fry tomatoes or other full sized tomato plant
1 Patio Pixie, Small Fry or Sugar Lump tomato	

Feeding

Roots are constantly taking nutrients from the soil, just as we eat food each day to keep our bodies functioning. The "food" that plants require are the same elements that we ingest, but plants need different proportions of those elements. Carbon, hydrogen and oxygen are "breathed" from the air, so we are not concerned with these. The three major nutrients plants take in from the soil are nitrogen, phosphorous and potassium. Equally as important, but needed only in tiny amounts, are the trace elements: calcium, copper, zinc, iron, manganese, magnesium, sulphur, boron, chlorine and cobalt.

A soil deficient in nitrogen will produce stunted, pale green foliage. An overdose will produce fast-growing, green-black foliage with few vegetables. Phosphorous deficiency will weaken the roots, causing the plants to grow flat on the ground rather than upright. Blossoms may fall off or not reach a mature size. Potassium deficiency will produce strong-looking stalks which are really weak, and vegetables which ripen before they reach a mature size. Yellow spots may develop between veins on lower leaves. Trace-element deficiencies show as yellow leaves or spots on foliage, mottled leaves, or tip edges dry and brittle.

Plants in containers demand more frequent feeding since the increased watering washes out the nutrients with the drainage water, leaving the plant with a fertilizer deficiency. Proper feeding will keep plants growing rather than merely existing.

In the spring and summer, weekly feeding with a vegetable fertilizer or special container gardening food should supply the plant adequately. Manufactured fertilizers have two advantages over organic matter or compost—the nutrients are readily available to plant roots, and they are less mess. But either organic or commercial fertilizers are fine as long as they supply the plant with its day to day needs.

Mulches

A mulch is nothing more than a protectant. It keeps stray weeds out and moisture in as well as moderating the soil temperature and breaking the pressure of water droplets on the soil surface. Common mulching materials include: straw, plastic, newspapers, ground

Without mulch, the soil surface disintigrates or crusts. Mulch prevents this and keeps the ground evenly moist while suffocating stray weeds.

corncobs, peat moss, sawdust, wood chips, nut shells, gravel, leaves and shredded bark.

Start adding mulch to your container when plants are 4 inches high. Prior to this, the mulch may smother the seedlings or rob them of light. Make sure the soil is damp so there is sufficient moisture underneath, then layer the mulch to a depth of 1-4 inches.

Mulches reduce water evaporation from 30-70 percent. The warming of the soil promotes earlier maturity and higher yields by lessening the loss of fruit through rot. The scorching rays of the sun are kept from overheating plant roots. Raindrops tend to cement the soil surface, but mulches will break the pressure of those drops. In winter, mulches will protect containers left outdoors from alternate freezing, thawing and heaving of the soil.

Staking

Staking plants on a stick, trellis or wall keeps the plants off the ground, away from insects and disease. Vining plants need tying to the support since they cling, but not tightly enough to withstand strong wind or heavy weight. When tying use strips of soft cloth or nylon stockings to prevent injury to stems. Tie the strip in a figure 8 as added protection, and make certain that the material isn't tied tightly around the stem.

Be sure to sink trellises or stakes deeply into the ground before planting so that plant roots are not injured. In hot climates, don't use metal frames or chicken wire. Foliage and plant tendrils will burn after touching the heated metal during the day. Use bamboo or wooden stakes or plastic support systems.

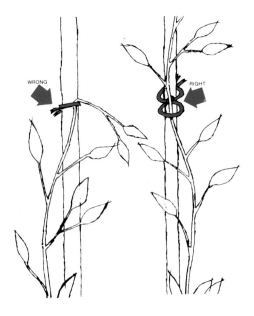

String or twist-ties around a plant will cut into the stem. Use cloth or nylon strips in a figure-8 around stakes and stems to reduce damage.

Using a trellis for sprawling vegetables will increase your garden space and yields. Never use metal materials—plants will fry.

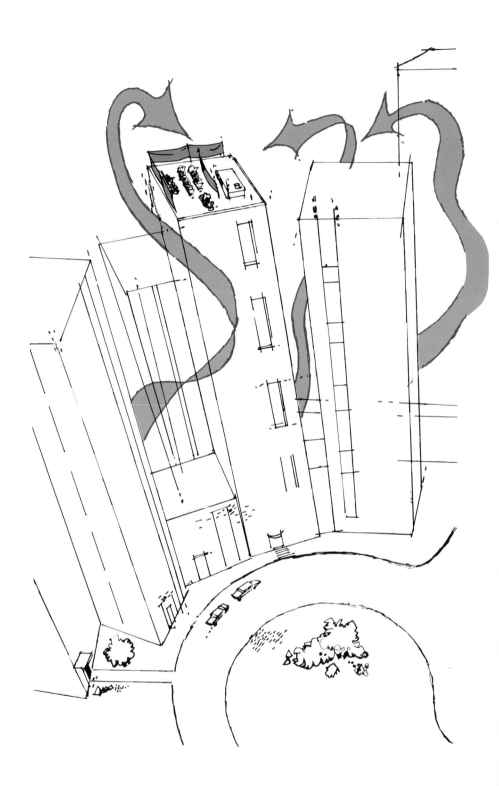

Protection

Plants outdoors are subject to detrimental natural forces such as wind, frost, insects and animals. Shelter containers away from these forces as much as possible.

Windbreaks made of clear fiberglass, awnings or screens will break the force of wind but permit air circulation. This is essential in urban areas where air is squeezed and accelerated through skyscraper canyons. A shingle or milk carton will break the force of wind.

Hot caps of clear plastic, styrofoam, plastic bleach bottles or coffee cans will keep the plants inside several degrees warmer than the outside night air. Remove the protection during the day or provide ventilation. If the weather turns warm, the covered plants may cook. An advantage of containerized plants is that they can be moved into a garage or house when there is danger of a frost.

Insects move from place to place and are liable to attack your plants no matter how hard you try to stop them. But it is easier to check containers for insects than it is an entire field. If you find undesirable bugs, you can first try picking them off. For flying insects, hose them off or try spraying with soapy water. If that doesn't work, use an organic botanical spray, make your own by squeezing the juice from garlic, onions or peppers, or use a chemical pesticide. Chemicals do the best job, but be sure the one you use is approved for food crops. Only Sevin, Diazinon and Malathion can be used on edible crops. Package labels will give approval information. Vegetables cannot be eaten within a time period after spraying, so check the label for each crop. Don't confuse non-acceptable insecticides with fungicides such as Captan which are safe. If in doubt—ask!

Aluminum strips strung on thin black thread between stakes will deter birds and keep them from landing. A net covering the entire tree or container will prevent birds from eating ripe fruit. Animals can be kept away by elevating containers off the ground or surrounding your container garden with a fence.

Harvesting

Recommendations for picking times can be found under each individual vegetable crop. To catch vegetables when the flavor and sugar is at its peak, pick them before they are completely mature and cook or freeze them immediately. Yields of all species are decreased if mature vegetables are left on the plant or vine. The plant is fooled into thinking it has enough seeds which will fall on the ground and begin new plants for the new year. It doesn't know that we are going to foil its motherly instincts by removing and eating its offspring. When vegetables are kept picked, the plant will continue to set fruit, hoping that some of its seeds will live until the following year to continue the family line.

High-rise gardens need extra protection from accelerated winds and heat currents rising from the pavement below.

2

Interesting to try

Variations of the basic
container gardening steps or
folklore practices are not
required by a plant in order to
grow, but can be fun
for you to try.

Companion planting

Some plants give off substances through their leaves and roots which are thought to affect other plants. Over the years, the aromas and exudates of plants have been observed and used to encourage better plant growth relationships as well as repel insects. Some of these compatibilities have been proven to be physical or chemical reactions—marigolds have a substance given off by their roots which repels nematodes (soil-borne worms), and corn may protect a short shade-loving plant. Others are folklore, passed on from generations of people who adhered to these guidelines faithfully. You can make your own judgments on their validity. But try a few first and see if garlic doesn't repel flying insects—it works at repelling people when you have it on your breath, doesn't it?

Marigolds		The foliage is said to repel bean beetles, tomato fruit worms, flea beetles and whitefly. The roots exude a substance which will kill nematodes in the soil. To be effective in the soil, they must be grown in the same spot for several years.
Nasturtiums		Reportedly they repel squash bugs from cucumbers, melons and squashes. Nasturtiums give radishes a great flavor.
Beans		Beans will thrive when planted beside carrots, cauliflower, cucumbers, corn and radishes. They dislike onions, beets, garlic, gladioli and sunflowers. Summer savory is a friend that repels bean beetles.

Beets		Beets do well with any plants as companions, but do better near lettuce, cabbage, onions and bush beans. Pole beans are the only vegetable that will stunt beet growth.
Cabbage		Strawberries, pole beans or tomatoes close by will discourage cabbage growth. Rosemary, mint, thyme and other aromatic herbs repel the cabbage worm and adult butterfly. Sage gives off camphor which also repels the cabbage moth.
Cauliflower		Aromatic herbs benefit cauliflower.

Carrots		Carrots dislike only dill, which is a relative. They grow well with Brussels sprouts, peas, cabbage, lettuce, radishes and chives. Leeks, sage and rosemary repel the carrot fly.
Corn		The addition of nitrogen to the soil by peas and beans enhances the growth of corn. Corn itself stimulates cucumbers, squash and melons.
Cucumbers		Cucumbers are one of the few vegetables that dislike the aromatic herbs. Likewise, they do not do well with potatoes. They prefer corn, cabbage, bush beans, lettuce or radishes. Radishes seem to scare cucumber beetles away from all the cucumber relatives.

Lettuce		Lettuce is aided by the root crops, especially beets and carrots. Onions and cabbage are helped along by lettuce growing in the same pot.
Melons		Corn and melons are good companions.
Onions		An oil from onions inhibits the growth of beans and peas. Onions like most other plants especially beets, cabbage, lettuce and summer savory.

Peas		Peas dislike onions, garlic and potatoes. The nitrogen peas provide the soil benefits most other plants. Carrots give off a root exudate that benefits peas. Around beans, cucumbers, corn and radishes, peas grow better than they would alone.
Peppers		Onions, carrots, tomatoes and eggplant are good neighbors.
Radishes		Pure in spirit, radishes seem to have no enemies. They favor neighbors like carrots, lettuce, peas, cucumbers, and pole beans. Plant nasturtiums close by for a better radish flavor.

Squash		Like pumpkins and melons, squashes like to grow with corn.
Tomatoes		Potatoes, dill and cabbage are unwelcome next to tomato plants. Onions, asparagus, and parsley stimulate their growth.
Basil		Basil repels flies and mosquitoes.

Catnip		Flea beetles are repelled while cats are attracted to catnip.
Chives		Chives seem to enhance the growth of carrots and tomatoes while repelling a collection of insects.
Garlic		The foul smell is a repellent to Japanese beetles, aphids, mosquitoes, caterpillars and sucking bugs. The aromatic oil seems to control some blight diseases.

Marjoram		Marjoram is credited with stimulating almost everything in the garden.
Mint		Mint repels the cabbage butterfly and ants.
Oregano		Similar to marjoram, oregano stimulates plant growth in general.

Rosemary		Rosemary repels the cabbage moth, bean beetles and carrot fly.
Sage		The camphor given off by sage is thought to repel the cabbage butterfly, bean beetle and carrot fly.
Summer Savory		Like rosemary and sage, savory repels the bean beetle. It is also helpful when planted beside onions.
Thyme		Thyme repels the cabbage worm.

Successive Cropping

For vegetables which mature fast or all at one time, weekly sowings of seed will insure a continuous crop throughout the summer. Carrots, beets, radishes, lettuce, spinach, endive, corn, peas and beans planted in this way will mature one week after the previously sown plants were picked, giving you vegetables until the first frost. Tomatoes, cucumbers, peppers and eggplant will keep producing on the same plants, so successive cropping is not necessary.

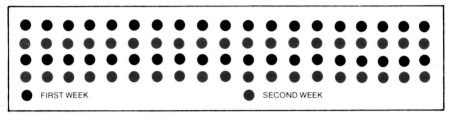

● FIRST WEEK   ● SECOND WEEK

Succession Planting

This is a variation of successive cropping. But after a vegetable like a quick-maturing radish is plucked out of the container, seed of another vegetable is sown in its place. Unlike successive cropping, succession uses the same amount of container space, you just have to wait for vegetables to ripen before replacing them.

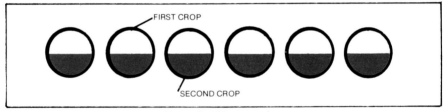

FIRST CROP

SECOND CROP

Catch Cropping

This is a system for thrifty space users. Fast-growing crops such as lettuce or green onions are planted between slower-growing crops such as eggplant. By the time you are ready to eat your green onions, the eggplant is getting ready to use that extra space—in the soil and above ground for expansion. Take care not to plant the different species too close together so the root system of the slower growing vegetable will not be damaged when the early-maturing crop is removed from the soil. By using a catch-cropping or interplanting system, large quantities of a variety of vegetables can be produced in a very small area.

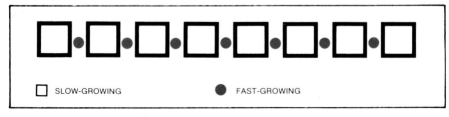

□ SLOW-GROWING   ● FAST-GROWING

Overwintering

The major difference between growing a plant in a container rather than in the ground is the soil temperature. If the container is not protected, the soil will freeze solidly and plants will die because they cannot get moisture. All plants still need some water in the winter, but if the soil is frozen, water will become ice crystals.

The surface, which is releasing heat from the soil to the air, surrounds the plant roots on all four sides rather than one. The temperature of the soil in a container is close to that of air temperature. Soils in a field have reserved heat further down in lower layers.

Sources of protection for your plant are mulches, microfoam or polyethylene tents. Wind barriers or snow do not provide adequate protection, but may reduce temperature fluctuations and desiccation.

Lay a 3-4 inch layer of mulch or newspaper over the container, then cover with a large cardboard box or tarpaulin. Unheated, but not freezing, porches or garages are suitable for unmulched tubs, especially for fruit trees and perennial plants.

Midget Vegetables

Midget vegetable varieties are extra early, space-saving vegetables bred to be one-half to one-quarter the plant and fruit size of normal vegetables. Container varieties on the other hand, have equally small plant parts, but they bear full-sized vegetables. You have to grow at least twice as many midget plants as a standard variety to get an equal yield, but anyone with a 4-or 6-inch flowerpot can produce cucumbers or tomatoes.

The only difference in culture is that the smaller pot sizes need more frequent watering and fertilizing.

Midget varieties which are now available include: cabbage, carrots, corn, cucumbers, eggplant, lettuce, cantaloupe, tomatoes and watermelon.

Indoor Gardening

Imagine the comments you'll get from admiring guests when you show them your floor-to-ceiling sweet potato vine after serving them a salad from your windowsill lettuce and tomato planters.

Some vegetables, such as the salad crops, can grow year-round indoors and produce a crop. Others are good for starting indoors for spring transplanting outdoors, or you can bring them inside to avoid the frost and extend your harvesting season.

The problem seems to be that root or leafy vegetables (spinach, radishes, carrots, beets, lettuce, endive, green onions and herbs) require much less light than the vine crops and other vegetables that continue to bear on the same plant. Using lights, tomatoes, cucumbers, and all other vegetables will grow, but need so much light intensity that you may have plants with bushy foliage which never blossom.

During the winter, plants growing close to windows should be moved away from the glass every night during cold weather. Newspaper laid against the glass will help keep the warm air from escaping at night. Transparent plastic bags placed over plants at night or during the day will confine precious humidity and heat. If there is condensation on your windows in the morning, those windowsills are a good place for your plants to take advantage of this extra humidity.

If you use a gas stove, watch for toxic effects on your plants. The symptoms are leaves and buds turning yellow and dropping.

Most plants seem to do best with 12-15 hours of light each day at a 65-70°F temperature. In order to receive this much light, electricity will have to supplement or replace winter sunlight. To flower and fruit, vegetables also need a period of darkness, so do not light 24 hours a day.

THE ELECTROMAGNETIC SPECTRUM

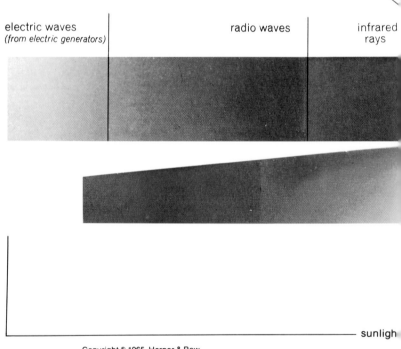

To use artificial lights, first understand what each type can provide and what plants require. Sunlight supplies the full spectrum of light—visible and invisible. Our electric lights can only duplicate a portion of that spectrum. A normal light bulb (incandescent) gives off red and far-red rays (invisible to our eyes). A fluorescent tube produces blue and red rays. Plants, not knowing what type of electric lights Thomas Edison would invent, have an absolute requirement for blue, red, and far red rays. They will grow under either type of light bulb, but most are prolific if they are shone upon by all three groups of rays.

To accomplish this, we can use a combination of a fluorescent tube with an incandescent bulb or use a plant grow-light which combines those two into one bulb. One cool-white fluorescent tube and one warm-white fluorescent tube can successfully be used for crops that do not require production of blossoms to obtain vegetables (salad crops). Place all plants within 6-8 inches of the light source. Move the tubes or plants as the seedlings grow in order to avoid scorched foliage.

nt

| ultraviolet rays | X rays | gamma rays | cosmic rays |

VISIBLE LIGHT SPECTRUM

3

Crops

Container gardening differs in many ways from conventional gardening in the ground. Step-by-step instructions for successful tub farming are given only for crops which are suitable for growing in pots.

You can grow any vegetable or fruit in a container—as long as you have a large enough container. Because most of us don't have enough space for gardening, plant breeders have developed plant varieties that are suitable for growing in pots, tubs or other limited spaces. Now you can grow watermelons that won't engulf your balcony, or start a midwestern cornfield mixed in with your petunias.

The actual size of container vegetables or fruits ranges from midget to beefsteak. The difference is that the plant itself is smaller, but much more efficient in the photosynthetic process.

The following recommendations are for tub-grown vegetables using container varieties. Keep in mind that some of this information is very different from outdoor gardening tips, geared exclusively to container growing. Recommendations are given for each crop on the ease of growing them indoors or out. Vegetables rated "excellent" are the easiest to grow, and produce abundantly.

PLANT	CONTAINER	YIELD	DEPTH TO PLANT SEED	DAYS TO MATURE PLANT
BEAN Warm-season crop **Outdoors:** excellent **Indoors:** poor **How to start:** seed Sleep movements	**Minimum container size for 1 plant:** 8 inches deep, 4 inches wide **Container varieties:** **Snap:** (bush) Tendercrop, Topcrop, Greensleeves, (bush wax) Pencil Pod Wax, Burpees Brittle Wax, (bush purple) Royalty (pole), Kentucky Wonder, Blue Lake, Ramona, **Lima:** Fordhook 242, Henderson Bush, King of the Garden	**Approximate yield per plant:** ¼ pound **Eventual Spacing:** **Snap:** Bush: 8 inches Pole: 9-12 inches **Lima:** 4-6 inches	**Depth to plant seed:** 1 inch in spring 2 inches in summer	**Days to mature vegetables:** **Snap:** Bush: 50-60 Pole: 60 **Lima:** 75-90 Plant eye to point downward

CULTURE AND HARVESTING

Culture

Beans can be divided into two groups—the snap beans and lima beans. Both of these groups come in two different growth habits—bush and pole.

Bush beans grow to 15-20 inches in height and mature in less than 60 days. Pole varieties grow to 5-8 feet in height and must be trained to a pole or trellis.

If you have unlimited vertical space, then the more plants you can get into the air on a trellis, the more food your beans will crank out.

Beans are heat lovers, so plant after the soil has warmed in the spring. This should be around the time when the later-leafing trees such as hickory and oak unfurl their foliage in the spring. Seeds will rot in cold soil, so if you have any doubts about the temperature, wait.

Soak the seeds in water overnight to soften the seed coat. Look for the seed "eye" on the edge of the bean. This is the opening through which the root will emerge. Drop the seed in a 1-inch hole, making sure the eye is pointing down. This will increase the yield for all bean varieties.

Cover with loose soil. A sprouting bean must pull its folded leaves (cotyledons) through the soil before spreading them in the air. Crusted or heavy soils resist the upward movement of the leaves, causing the shoots to break.

Water the plants frequently by soaking the soil instead of sprinkling. Bacterial diseases and mildew are encouraged by moist foliage. Lack of moisture will cause the plants to produce "pollywogs." The first few seeds develop normally and the rest of the pod shrivels, making it look like a tadpole.

Pole beans need some type of support—a trellis, pole, drainpipe, tree strump, string fence or anything vertical. You can get more beans from a pole variety than from a bush variety.

One of the more unusual natural movements of plants are the sleep movements. Plants such as clover, oxalis, some weeds and beans "go to sleep" at night. During the day the leaves grow in a horizontal position, then begin to droop and close in the evening, not rising again until the next morning.

Beans are difficult to grow indoors under lights. They will have good vegetative growth, but usually fail to produce a crop.

Harvesting

Look for the smoothness and greenness of the pods. Snap beans should be 3 inches long. When picking, hold the stem and pluck off the pod. This prevents breaking off stems and destroying the plant. Beans are past their prime when color fades and seeds begin to show through, giving a corrugated appearance to the pod. Lima beans should have a slight corrugated look.

If the plants look healthy but you never get much of a crop, be sure there are no mature pods remaining on the plant. Even a few old pods fool the plants into thinking their job is done for the season. They will not produce new pods for a new crop.

Pole beans need support

PLANT	CONTAINER	YIELD	DEPTH TO PLANT SEED	DAYS TO MATURE PLANT
BEET Cool-season crop **Outdoors:** excellent **Indoors:** excellent **How to start:** seed	**Minimum container size for 1 plant:** 2 inches wide, 2 inches deep **Container varieties:** Detroit Dark Red, Early Wonder, Ruby Queen (for greens): Sugar Beets, Green Top Bunching	**Approximate yield per plant:** 1 beet **Eventual Spacing:** 2 inches	**Depth to plant seed:** ½ inch	**Days to mature vegetables:** 55-6

Beet seeds sprout in clusters, and need to be thinned

CULTURE AND HARVESTING

Culture

Beets are star performers in containers. They grow like mad but don't take much room. They do equally well indoors or out. Another bonus is that both roots and leaves can be eaten.

Generally, beets like cool weather, although they are fairly tolerant of a wide temperature range. Inside, plant beets anytime.

The seeds of beets come in clusters, so it's necessary to soak them in water and separate individual seeds before planting. If they aren't separated, the seeds will germinate in groups, causing crowding.

Scatter the seed 1 inch apart and ½ inch deep. Later thin to a distance of 2 inches.

Harvesting

Begin pulling beets when they are 1 inch across. At 2 inches they have an excellent flavor, but when they reach 3 inches, they become tough and woody. They are past their prime when the lower leaves turn yellow.

PLANT	CONTAINER	YIELD	DEPTH TO PLANT SEED	DAYS TO MATURE PLANT
BROCCOLI Cool-season crop **Outdoors:** good **Indoors:** poor **How to start:** transplants or seeds	**Minimum container size for 1 plant:** 5 gal. of soil or a 12-inch diameter pot **Container varieties:** Green Comet, Spartan Early, Italian Green Sprouting, De Cicco	**Approximate yield per plant:** 1 pound **Eventual spacing:** 12-18 inches	Depth to plant seed: ¼ inch	Days to mature vegetables: 75-9

CULTURE AND HARVESTING

Culture

Broccoli, like other members of the cabbage family, will take over your container. It can grow to 3-4 feet in height and branch nearly as wide.

To start indoors, sow seed 1/4 inch deep in peat pots, about 6 weeks before you intend to transplant. Under lights it will grow up to 1 foot but won't mature. A better method is to set outdoors when 6-7 inches high.

Broccoli can be a problem since it is so sensitive to heat. Set your seedlings or nursery transplants outdoors in very early spring or in mid-summer. By the time the plants mature, the weather will still be cool enough for good vegetable development.

In mild climates, winter crops can be grown successfully. From 70 to 90 days of cool weather are needed to form heads.

Push along its growth with frequent applications of high-nitrogen (10-10-10) plant food.

Harvesting

Cut off the top cluster while the buds are still tight, hard and green. Include 5-6 inches of the stem and leaves with the head. The plant will continue to send up edible clusters after the central head is cut. To encourage more crops, harvest the side clusters as soon as they are ripe.

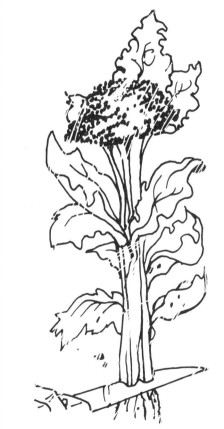

Harvest brocolli head and 6 inches of stem

PLANT	CONTAINER	YIELD	DEPTH TO PLANT SEED	DAYS TO MATURE PLANT
BRUSSELS SPROUTS Cool-season crop **Outdoors:** good **Indoors:** excellent **How to start:** transplants or seed	**Minimum container size for 1 plant:** 5 gal. of soil or a 12-inch diameter pot **Container varieties:** Jade Cross Hybrid, Long Island Improved	**Approximate yield per plant:** 75-100 sprouts **Eventual spacing:** 12-18 inches	**Depth to plant seed:** ½ inch	**Days to mature vegetables:** 80-90

CULTURE AND HARVESTING

Culture

The plant is really a vertical cabbage that produces many tiny heads upright along the stem instead of just one big head on the ground.

Brussels sprouts do not do well in a hot, dry climate. Ideal growth occurs in areas that have summer fog, or moist air and daytime temperatures around 65°

From seed, plants can be started indoors in peat pots 6 weeks before transplanting. Since the sprouts require 4-5 months from seeding time to maturity, set out started seedlings or nursery transplants in early summer. This allows them to come to full maturity in cooler fall weather. As the plants grow, remove all excess leaves except for those at the top of the plant.

Harvesting

Once the sprouts begin appearing, you'll think the plant will never quit! Pick the lowest sprouts when they are 1 to 1½ inches in diameter. Break off any leaves below the sprout. Mild frost improves the flavor, so don't worry about bringing the plant indoors in the fall. Plants will continue to produce during the winter months in southern states.

PLANT	CONTAINER	YIELD	DEPTH TO PLANT SEED	DAYS TO MATURE PLANT
CABBAGE Cool-season crop **Outdoors:** good **Indoors:** poor **How to start:** transplants or seed	**Minimum container size for 1 plant:** 3 gal. of soil or a 10-inch diameter pot **Container varieties:** (early) Early Jersey Wakefield, Copenhagen Market, Marion Market, (late) Danish Ballhead, (red) Red Acre, Ruby Ball Hybrid, (decorative) Savoy King, (midget) Dwarf Morden, Baby Head.	**Approximate yield per plant:** 1 head **Eventual spacing:** 12-20 inches	**Depth to plant seed:** ½ inch	**Days to mature vegetables:** 60-10

CULTURE AND HARVESTING

Culture

Cabbage comes in a range of sizes and colors to please everyone—green, purple, red, decorative and midget. To show them off to full advantage, plant one head per container.

From seed, plant ½ inch deep in flats or peat pots 6 weeks before you intend to plant in open ground outdoors. Plants can be set out in early spring or late summer.

Cabbage needs a large amount of nutrients from the soil in a constant supply. Feed with a vegetable plant food twice each week.

Never plant cabbage in the same container as cauliflower, Brussels sprouts, broccoli, kohrabi, Chinese cabbage, kale or collards. Diseases can be transferred among any of these cabbage relatives. Buy seed or transplants of disease-resistant varieties.

Splitting of the head is common with cabbage if it matures in warm weather. Hold off water or twist the plant to break off some of the roots.

Harvesting

Pick heads as soon as they feel solid and are at least 4" in diameter. Continue until the heads are 6-10 inches.

PLANT	CONTAINER	YIELD	DEPTH TO PLANT SEED	DAYS TO MATURE PLANT
CARROT Cool-season crop **Outdoors:** excellent **Indoors:** good **How to start:** seed	**Minimum container size for 1 plant:** 1 inch wide, 4 inches deep **Container varieties:** Little Finger, Ox-Heart, Baby Finger, Royal Chantenay, Red Cored Chantenay, Spartan Bonus, Nantes, Short 'N Sweet, Gold Pak	**Approximate yield per plant:** 1 carrot **Eventual spacing:** 1-2 inches	**Depth to plant seed:** ½ inch	**Days to mature vegetables:** 65-7

CULTURE AND HARVESTING

Culture

Carrots are a near-perfect crop to grow in containers. They take very little room, will not spoil if they stay in the ground a long time, are somewhat indifferent to temperature, and give us a vegetable packed with vitamins A, B1, B2, C, sugars and iron. They are tolerant of gardening mistakes.

An artificial soil mix is preferred because it is loose, free of clods and permits the rapid growth that makes carrots tender and sweet. A heavy clay soil or one with too much compost will cause the carrot to fork.

Carrots can be planted any time of year, although they prefer cool temperatures. Sow seed $\frac{1}{2}$ inch apart in all directions in a permanent container. Cover with $\frac{1}{2}$ inch of soil. The seeds are slow to germinate, so place a plastic sheet over the top to trap moisture and heat. As soon as the sprouts appear, remove the plastic.

The seedlings at first look like feathery weeds, so be careful not to pluck them out too soon.

Fast growth and adequate water are necessary. Don't let carrots dry out or growth will be retarded and a strong flavor will develop.

If the pot is less than 4 inches, the carrot will touch the bottom and never mature. Be sure your pot is deep enough for the variety you are growing.

No root but lots of foliage is due to crowding. Thin the plants to the spacing indicated on the seed packet.

Harvesting

The best-tasting carrots are small "finger" carrots. When the root becomes too big, the core may be woody. Pull carrots when they are 1-1$\frac{1}{2}$ inches in diameter and 3-4 inches long.

PLANT	CONTAINER	YIELD	DEPTH TO PLANT SEED	DAYS TO MATURE PLANT
CAULIFLOWER Cool-season crop **Outdoors:** fair **Indoors:** poor **How to start:** transplants or seeds	**Minimum container size for 1 plant:** 5 gal. of soil or a 12-inch diameter pot **Container varieties:** Early Snowball, Snow King Hybrid, Snow Crown Hybrid, Purple Head	**Approximate yield per plant:** 1 head **Eventual spacing:** 18 inches	**Depth to plant seed:** ½ inch	**Days to mature vegetables:** 50-60 days

CULTURE AND HARVESTING

Culture

Cauliflower is a slow-growing, cool-weather vegetable. If your summers are at all hot, plant in the late summer for a fall harvest.

From seed, cauliflower takes 50 days before the plants are ready to transplant. For fall crops, seeds can be sown outside in May or June. Plant 3-4 seeds $\frac{1}{2}$ inch deep, and later thin to the one strongest plant. For best results, buy nursery transplants.

In areas with mild winters, cauliflower can be grown as a winter crop. Plants do not like temperatures above 80°F or below 30°F, so make sure they are protected during extreme fluctuations.

Did you ever wonder how some heads of cauliflower stayed a bright white even after sitting in your refrigerator for days, while others were always yellow? The white heads have been blanched while they were growing. To do this, pull the outer leaves over the head, tying them loosely at the top with a string or rubber band. This shields the head from the sun and keeps it a pure white color. Imagine the labor involved in tying each head in a commercial field!

Harvesting

When the curds have filled out on the head, it is ready for picking.

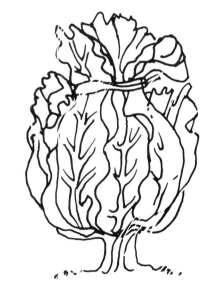

Blanching a cauliflower head

PLANT	CONTAINER	YIELD	DEPTH TO PLANT SEED	DAYS TO MATURE PLANT
CORN Warm-season crop **Outdoors:** good **Indoors:** poor **How to start:** seed	**Minimum container size for 1 plant:** 8 inches deep, 4 inches wide. Corn should be planted in groups of at least 12 plants, in a container at least 21 inches in diameter **Container varieties:** Early Sunglow, Butterfinger, Earliking, Seneca Chief, Illinichief, (white) Silver Sweet, (bicolor) Honey and Cream, Sugar and Gold, Butter and Sugar, (midget) Golden Midget	**Approximate yield per plant:** 1-2 ears **Eventual spacing:** 8-12 inches	**Depth to plant seed:** 1 inch	**Days to mature vegetables:** 60-8

CULTURE AND HARVESTING

Culture

Your yield will not be more than 1 or 2 ears per plant, but you may decide it is fun to have a cornfield in a tub.

Corn is a heat lover and a very gregarious vegetable. It is wind pollinated which means the plants must be grown close together since the pollen cannot float very far. About a dozen plants of one variety should be grown in a tub or several tubs sitting next to each other. Each kernel on an ear must be pollinated or it will shrivel and leave a hole on the cob. If another variety of corn is being grown nearby, the pollen may drift and you will have mixed kernels on one ear. Wet or extremely hot weather will also interfere with pollination.

The variety of corn goes from the standard yellow to white, bicolor, Indian corn, strawberry and popcorn. All can be grown in containers, but the most successful are those that will grow only to a 4-6 foot height, or true midget varieties.

Plant seeds 4 inches apart and thin to a distance of 8-12 inches apart when the seedlings are 6 inches tall.

Adequate watering is essential after the plants are 3-4 inches tall. It is difficult to overwater, and disastrous not to supply enough, so pour it on!

In very hot, dry weather the leaves may roll or curl. The plants are giving off water essentially they are sweating as you and I do) faster than the roots can absorb it. Keep the soil moist and the leaves will return to normal.

Indoors, it is possible to grow corn in one large tub. Be sure to put it in a south window for maximum light.

Feed corn with a vegetable fertilizer every week.

Harvesting

Corn must be picked within a 72-hour period for the best flavor—that doesn't leave much room for error or vacations.

Three weeks after you see the pollen fly, pull down a husk and prick a kernel with your thumbnail. If the juice is watery, wait a few days. If it's just right, it will squirt a milky juice. If the juice has the consistency of toothpaste, you're too late. As soon as an ear is picked, the sugar begins to turn to starch. If you wait too long to cook or freeze it, only the cattle will enjoy the flavor. Pop it into boiling water immediately or drop the ears in ice water and store in the refrigerator. If the ears are past their prime, use them for chowder or creamed corn.

PLANT	CONTAINER	YIELD	DEPTH TO PLANT SEED	DAYS TO MATURE PLANT
CUCUMBER Warm-season crop **Outdoors:** excellent **Indoors:** poor **How to start:** seeds or transplants	**Minimum container size for 1 plant:** 2 gal. of soil or an 8-inch diameter pot. **Container varieties:** Pot Luck, Patio Pik, Burpless Early Pik, Crispy Salty, Tiny Dill Cuke	**Approximate yield per plant:** 10-12 cucumbers **Eventual spacing:** 4 inches for vertical growing	**Depth to plant seed:** 1 inch	**Days to mature vegetables:** 50-

Left: pickling cucumber
Above: slicing cucumber

Culture

The best way to grow container cucumbers is up in the air. Trained on a trellis or strings, the runners won't take over all the available space around them and will produce as much as 5 times the amount as would rambling vines. An added bonus is that the leaves will not remain in contact with water or damp earth which promotes disease infection.

For a head start on the season, sow seeds indoors in peat pots or flats. Plant ½ inch deep in the soil. Seeds should be started no more than 2-4 weeks before transplanting. Cucumbers are heat lovers so wait until a week after final frost date for outdoor planting. Then seeds can be placed 1 inch deep and 4 inches apart in a container.

Cucumbers are like humans—there are male and female flowers, and only females will produce the vegetable. The first 15-20 flowers that you see are males, and will fall off. The flowers produced after these will give you cucumbers.

Make sure the plant never dries out or growth and vegetable production will be severely affected.

If your plants are trained to grow into the air, support the cucumber with a cloth sling tied to the support frame. This will ease the strain and weight the plant must bear.

To produce more and superior fruits, pinch off the growing tip of the leading shoot after it has produced 6-8 leaves. This encourages the plant to branch and produce more fruit-bearing vines.

Indoors, cucumbers can be grown successfully during the winter. Since the plants are normally pollinated by the wind, transfer the pollen with your fingertips from male to female flowers. Female flowers have a tiny cucumber forming below the blossom. If pollination does not occur, the flowers will fall off and no cucumbers will develop.

If you can convince your dinner guests the skin on a cucumber is acceptable, leave it on. There is magnesium deposited under the skin which counteracts the bitterness and prevents burping.

Harvesting

Pick cucumbers before they turn yellow. At this stage the seeds become large and tough. Keep picking the fruit frequently. If mature fruits are left on the vines, fewer flowers will be produced, giving you fewer fruits later. Cucumbers for sweet pickles should be 3 inches long, dills 6 inches, slicing and fresh 8 inches.

Male blossom (left), female blossom (right)

PLANT	CONTAINER	YIELD	DEPTH TO PLANT SEED	DAYS TO MATURE PLANT
EGGPLANT Warm-season crop **Outdoors:** good **Indoors:** fair **How to start:** transplants or seed	**Minimum container size for 1 plant:** 5 gal. of soil or a 12-inch diameter tub **Container varieties:** Slim Jim, Ichiban, Black Beauty, Long Tom, Jersey King Hybrid	**Approximate yield per plant:** 4-8 eggplants **Eventual spacing:** 12 inches	**Depth to plant seed:** ¼-½ inch	**Days to mature vegetables:** 60-8 after transplanti

CULTURE AND HARVESTING

Culture

Eggplants are slow-growing, heat-loving plants. Cool weather slows them down.

Although the plant roots are fragile and do not transplant well, it is possible to start seeds indoors. Sow 2-3 seeds per peat pot or flat, cover to a depth of $\frac{1}{4}$ inch. Some seed takes 3 or more weeks to germinate when the soil temperature is at least 75°F, but better at 80-90°F. It may take another 8-10 weeks before they are large enough to transplant, so be sure to start early. Transplant a week after the last average spring frost date.

Once transplanted, eggplant needs regular watering and 3-4 additional feedings of fertilizer. In a climate that is too cool for eggplant, the reflected heat from a wall or black plastic hung behind the plant can supply the plant all the extra heat it needs to produce fruit.

Indoors, eggplant will grow under fluorescent lights at temperatures of 65-70°F. With enough supplemental light, fruit will be produced.

Harvesting

Fruits should be picked at 4-6 inches while they are still dark purple and shiny. When they lose their glossy shine, the eggplants will be tough. Be sure to keep picking fruits so that the plant will continue to bear.

PLANT	CONTAINER	YIELD	DEPTH TO PLANT SEED	DAYS TO MATURE PLANT
ENDIVE Cool-season crop **Outdoors:** excellent **Indoors:** excellent **How to start:** seed	**Minimum container size for 1 plant:** 6 inches wide, 6 inches deep **Container varieties:** Broad-leaved, Batavian, Salad King	**Approximate yield per plant:** 1 head **Eventual spacing:** 10 inches	**Depth to plant seed:** $1/4$-$1/2$ inch	**Days to mature vegetables:** 90

CULTURE AND HARVESTING

Culture

Endive is great as a lettuce substitute because it is more heat and cold resistant. It won't bolt and go to seed in the summer and will stand frost. Plant the same as you would lettuce.

The flavor will improve with cool weather and blanching. To blanch, gather the outer leaves and tie them loosely with a string or a rubber band. Be sure the central leaves are dry or rot may occur. It takes 2 weeks to make the heart leaves mild and tender.

Harvesting

Pick the leaves after blanching and use as you would lettuce.

PLANT	CONTAINER	YIELD	DEPTH TO PLANT SEED	DAYS TO MATURE PLANT
LETTUCE Cool-season crop **Outdoors:** excellent **Indoors:** excellent **How to start:** seed or transplants	**Minimum container size for 1 plant:** 8 inches wide, 6 inches deep **Container varieties:** Oak Leaf, Buttercrunch, Salad Bowl, Romaine, Dark Green Boston, Ruby, Bibb, Tendercrunch	**Approximate yield per plant:** 1 head **Eventual spacing:** 10 inches	Depth to plant seed: $\frac{1}{4}$-$\frac{1}{2}$	**Days to mature vegetables:** Head: 80-85 Bibb: 65-80 Romaine: 70-80 Loose Leaf: 40-4

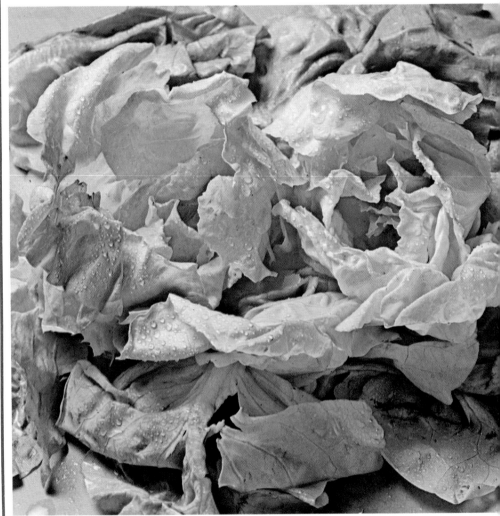

CULTURE AND HARVESTING

Culture

Lettuce is so versatile it will do extremely well in small containers, on a windowsill or under lights. Of the 4 general types (head, Romaine, Bibb and leaf), the leaf varieties are the best for containers. Their growing season is shorter than the others.

Leaf lettuce needs no transplanting since thinnings can be eaten in 3 weeks. Or for head lettuce, seeds can be planted 1/4 to 1/2 inch deep in pots or flats indoors about 2 weeks before the last frost, then set outside. Lettuce will tolerate light frost. Space head lettuce 10 inches between plants, Bibb 4-5, follow seed packet directions for Romaine and leaf lettuce.

For leaf lettuce grown indoors year-round, scatter seeds 1 inch apart and cover with 1/4 inch of soil. A miniature "lawn of lettuce" will provide enough for salads for weeks. Leave 6-8 plants to mature.

Be sure to use varieties that are slow to bolt. *Buttercrunch* is a good choice. In hot areas, lettuce becomes bitter and goes to seed—referred to as bolting. Give plants protection with a gauze frame, bamboo shade in front of indoor plants, or use a wooden shingle in front of plants to shield from the sun's rays. If protection does not work, discard the plant or keep it watered until the cooler fall weather. It will reseed itself to produce a new crop.

Lettuce grown under lights grows so rapidly it must have a weekly feeding or the leaves will turn yellow.

Harvesting

Pick the outer leaves of lettuce at any stage before they become yellow and bitter. Head lettuce should be picked while the leaves are compact and crisp.

A shingle shields lettuce from excessive sun and heat

PLANT	CONTAINER	YIELD	DEPTH TO PLANT SEED	DAYS TO MATURE PLANT
MELON Warm-season crop **Outdoors:** fair **Indoors:** poor **How to start:** seed or transplants	**Minimum container size for one plant:** 5 gallons of soil or a 12-inch diameter tub **Container Varieties:** (cantaloupe) Saticoy Hybrid, Gold Star, Harper's Hybrid (crenshaw) Early Crenshaw (honeydew) Honey Mist (watermelon) Crimson Sweet, Charleston Gray (midget) Minnesota Midget Muskmelon, New Hampshire Midget and Sugar Baby.	**Approximate yield per plant:** muskmelons: 2-4 watermelons: 2-3 **Eventual spacing:** 12 inches	**Depth to plant seed:** 1 inch	**Days to mature vegetables:** 70-9?

A sling helps supp?
the melon's weigh?

CULTURE AND HARVESTING

Culture

Watermelon is easy to distinguish, but after that, what is really the difference between muskmelon and cantaloupe? The term muskmelon includes cantaloupe, casaba, crenshaw, persian, banana and honeydew melons. Cantaloupes have deep orange flesh with a netted outside rind; crenshaw are pear-shaped with yellow skin and a light orange flesh; casaba are a wrinkled yellow with white flesh; honeydews have a smooth creamy rind with white and green; persian are green with a smooth netting on the skin and deep orange flesh; bananas are long, slender and have a yellow or green rind with deep orange flesh; watermelon may fool you with its pink or yellow flesh, but its two-tone green stripes on the rind are a give away.

For containers, train your melon vines up a trellis, or use a midget variety. Each vine will produce shoots 6-10 feet long so provide ample space.

Melons are hot-weather plants which can be sown outside in late spring or started indoors and transplanted when they are 2-3 inches high. Melon seeds need 80^0F temperature to germinate, so put flats or pots on a radiator, or possibly the top of a refrigerator if it is warm.

After transplanting, train the stems of your vine up a support system and tie a cloth sling around each melon so that its weight will not pull the vine down or break it. Feed the vines with a vegetable plant food at least once or twice during the growing season. Give them steady watering for good fruit development.

Harvesting

Melons will not develop additional sugar after they are picked. They will soften but never become sweet. Cantaloupes are ready when the stem breaks away easily with slight pressure. For Crenshaw, sniff the blossom end. If the aroma is sweet and fruity, it is ripe. Honey Dew and Casaba rinds should have turned completely yellow before picking. You have to have a well-trained ear to pick watermelons. A dull thump means they're ready. A ring or bong means they're still immature, although as they get hot late in the day it's hard to distinguish a thump from a bong. Most varieties of watermelon will turn yellow on the surface touching the ground indicating ripeness.

PLANT	CONTAINER	YIELD	DEPTH TO PLANT SEED	DAYS TO MATURE PLANT
ONION Cool-season crop **Outdoors:** excellent **Indoors:** good **How to start:** seed, transplants, sets	**Minimum container size for one plant:** 3 inches wide, 12 inches deep **Container Varieties:** White Sweet Spanish, Yellow Sweet Spanish, Southport White Globe, Southport Red Globe, Beltsville Bunching.	**Approximate yield per plant:** 1 onion **Eventual spacing:** Green onions-1 inch Bulb onions-3 inches	**Depth to plant seed:** ¼ inch	Days to mature vegetables: 65-1

CULTURE AND HARVESTING

Culture

Without onions, most food, even glorious hamburgers, would taste flat. The onion family includes green onions, bulbing onions, garlic, leeks, shallots and chives. All share oils in the plant parts which give onions their pungent taste and unmistakable odor.

To start onions from seed, plant one inch apart and cover with $\frac{1}{4}$ inch of soil. Any variety can be grown and pulled up as green onions. Thin to a 3-inch spacing for growing on as bulb onions. Seedlings or sets (tiny bulbs) are easier to handle. They should be planted 1-2 inches apart and later thinned to a 3-inch distance.

Onions should be given steady watering—never let the soil dry out. Give them weekly doses of vegetable plant food throughout the growing season.

For indoor gardeners, keep onions between 60-70°F. Lighting them 12 hours a day will cause the bulb to enlarge. Garlic lovers can stick a toothpick into a clove of garlic and suspend in a glass of water. Just snip off the green shoots when needed.

When the tops of the onion begin to dry and turn yellow, bend them parallel to the ground or break them. This restricts the flow of sap and concentrates all the growing energy to the bulb.

Harvesting

For bulbing types, after the tops are dead, dig up the bulbs and let them dry for a few days before storing.

Green onions can be harvested as special varieties or immature bulbing types 20-30 days after planting.

Before harvesting, bend onion stems parallel to the ground

PLANT	CONTAINER	YIELD	DEPTH TO PLANT SEED	DAYS TO MATURE PLANT
PEA Cool-season crop **Outdoors:** good **Indoors:** good **How to start:** seed	**Minimum container size for one plant:** 6-inch long box **Container Varieties:** Alaska, Little Marvel, Frosty, Green Arrow, (snow peas) Dwarf Gray Sugar, Burpee Sweet Pod, (cowpeas) Early Ramshorn Black Eye.	**Approximate yield per plant:** ⅛ pound **Eventual spacing:** 6 inches	**Depth to plant seed:** 2 inches	**Days to mature vegetables:** 55-7

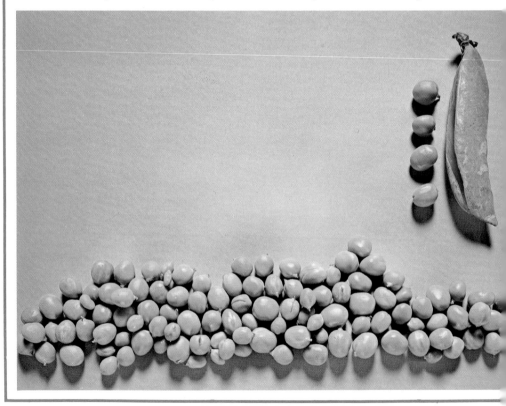

CULTURE AND HARVESTING

Culture

Peas in pots are not high-yielding, so many plants need to be grown. The plants should be grown on a trellis or chicken wire. The advantages are numerous. Peas produce such a mass of vegetation they would soon sprawl over other containers. The flowers get lost in the mass and are not pollinated adequately, resulting in the pods being only partially filled. As they grow, the pods need full exposure to the sun for development. Horizontal stems retard the flow of sap to the pods and make good hiding places for insects and diseased leaves.

Green peas cannot be grown successfully in states with warm climates since spring comes on too quickly and too warm, cheating the peas of a period of slow, crisp, cool growth. In these areas use early maturing varieties or substitute cowpeas or blackeyed peas.

Plant early in the spring directly into containers about 4-6 weeks before the last frost date. Long troughs or planter boxes are best. Keep them well watered after germination. Sow seeds at weekly intervals to harvest a continuous crop. Peas appreciate a vegetable fertilizer with a high potassium content.

If you have enough space indoors, peas are prolific when grown under lights. The number of vines required to produce a crop is usually impractical, but the growth is impressive as a house plant or even used as living room dividers!

Harvesting

Pick off the plump lower pods in the morning. Shell the peas and place in cool water in the refrigerator. Ripe pods should be kept picked to keep the plants producing steadily.

Peas must be trellised to receive maximum sunlight

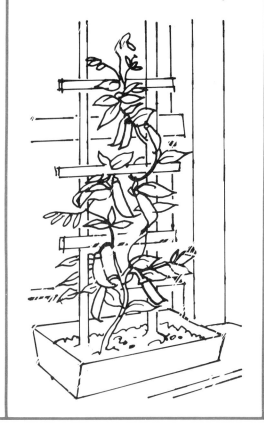

77

PLANT	CONTAINER	YIELD	DEPTH TO PLANT SEED	DAYS TO MATURE PLANT
PEPPER Warm-season crop **Outdoors:** excellent **Indoors:** fair **How to start:** transplants or seed	**Minimum container size for one plant:** 2 gallons of soil **Container Varieties:** (sweet) Bell Boy, Keystone Resistant, Yolo Wonder, (hot) Red Cherry, Long Red Cayenne, Jalapeno	**Approximate yield per plant:** 3-4 peppers **Eventual spacing:** 24 inches	**Depth to plant seed:** ½ inch	**Days to mature vegetables:** 65-8 after transplant

CULTURE AND HARVESTING

Culture

Peppers, like their tomato, eggplant, and potato relatives, attract the same bugs, and also like to bask in the heat. If temperatures fall below 60° F or rise above 90° F, they stubbornly refuse to set fruit. They are well suited for containers, since bringing them inside on a cool night or sweltering day will cure their fruit-setting problems.

From seed, start indoors, 2-4 seeds per pot about 10 weeks before you will transplant outdoors. Once outside, make sure the plants are watered and fed with a vegetable fertilizer weekly. In windy areas, staking the plants will protect the stems from breaking.

Harvesting

Pick sweet peppers when they are firm, crisp and still green. They are past their prime when the pepper becomes an overall red and skin becomes leathery. Allow hot peppers to become a bright red.

PLANT	CONTAINER	YIELD	DEPTH TO PLANT SEED	DAYS TO MATURE PLANT
RADISH Cool-season crop **Outdoors:** excellent **Indoors:** excellent **How to start:** seed	**Minimum container size for one plant:** 1 inch wide, 4 inches deep **Container Varieties:** Cherry Belle, Scarlet Globe, Icicle	**Approximate yield per plant:** 1 radish **Eventual spacing:** 1-2 inches	Depth to plant seed: ½ inch	Days to mature vegetables: 20-30

CULTURE AND HARVESTING

CULTURE

The radish is fast and fool-proof. Translated from Latin, "easily reared" is not only a name but a clue to how easy radishes are to cultivate. All varieties mature in a very short time after sowing. Planting seeds at weekly intervals will give you continuous crops all summer.

Being a cool weather crop, radishes don't do quite as well during mid-summer. After the heat wave has passed, continue sowing at weekly intervals. Radishes will continue to mature until a heavy, killing frost stops all growth.

In the late fall or winter, your radishes may become bottomless. The short day length is responsible for this. Bring the containers indoors and put the radishes under lights in the evening to extend the day length period.

HARVESTING

Radishes can be pulled at any time, preferably while still young and fairly small. Full maturity is reached in 20-30 days. After this they become pithy and bitter.

PLANT	CONTAINER	YIELD	DEPTH TO PLANT SEED	DAYS TO MATURE PLANT
SPINACH Cool-season crop **Outdoors:** good **Indoors:** good **How to start:** seed	**Minimum container size for one plant:** 4 inches wide, 4 inches deep **Container varieties:** Melody, Long Standing Bloomsdale, America	**Approximate yield per plant:** ¼ - ½ pound **Eventual spacing:** 5-6 inches	**Depth to plant seed:** ½ inch	**Days to mature vegetables:** 40-5

CULTURE AND HARVESTING

Culture

Spinach comes to us from Iran—no doubt in cans on board Popeye's sailing ship. The fresh leaves are used as a substitute for lettuce in salads while supplying you with the same amount of vitamin A as carrots—the vitamin linked with good vision. Spinach also contains iron, which is supposedly where Popeye got his strength—or did it come from the metal in the cans he swallowed whole?

This fast-growing crop matures in 6 weeks and quickly goes to seed. It should be grown in the spring or fall to prevent a bitter flavor.

Sow seeds 2 inches apart and later thin to a distance of 6 inches. Feed weekly with a vegetable fertilizer. Indoors, keep the temperature around 50-65° F.

Harvesting

When the outer leaves are 3 inches long, begin picking them as needed. The inner leaves then have a chance to develop and become the next crop. As soon as you see flower buds forming, harvest all the leaves. If you don't, they will become too bitter to eat as the plant goes to seed.

PLANT	CONTAINER	YIELD	DEPTH TO PLANT SEED	DAYS TO MATURE PLANT
SQUASH Warm-season crop **Outdoors:** good **Indoors:** poor **How to start:** seed or transplants	Minimum **container size for one plant:** 5 gallons of soil or a 12-inch diameter tub **Container Varieties:** (summer squash) Aristrocrat, Chefini, Greyzini, Hybrid Zucchini, Patty Pan, Scallopini (winter squash) Gold Nugget, Table King, Banana	**Approximate yield per plant:** summer squash: 10-20 winter squash: 8-10 **Eventual spacing:** 16-24 inches	Depth to plant **seed:** ½ inch	Days to mature vegetables: 50-1

84

Culture

Squashes can be divided into two groups by the time required for them to ripen. The summer squashes include the zucchini, crookneck, pattypan or scallop types. Winter squashes—which actually ripen in the fall—include acorn, butternut and Hubbard squashes. The flesh of summer squash is white or yellow, while that of winter squash is orange. Pumpkins are related to squashes and their growth and appearance are similar.

All squashes and pumpkins should be grown vertically against a trellis or wall. The vining types need up to 10 feet of climbing room, which is a good reason to put your vines up in the air rather than making your container a space-grabbing octopus.

A cloth sling tied around the squash and attached to the trellis will support the weight of the squash without pulling down the vine.

Start seeds indoors around a 65-70° F temperature in individual peat pots. Direct seeding outdoors is preferred, but wait unitl air temperature regularly stays above 55° F.

Harvesting

Summer squash can be harvested when fruits are only 2 inches long and until the skin becomes tough. Winter squash should be fully mature before picking. Leave them on the vines until the shells are hardened. Without fully ripening, the winter squashes will not store well through the winter.

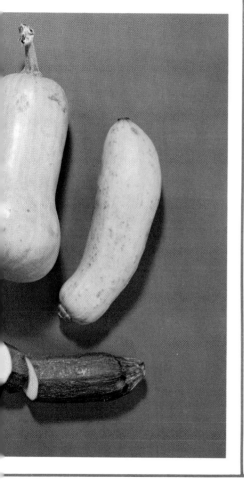

PLANT	CONTAINER	YIELD	DEPTH TO PLANT SEED	DAYS TO MATURE PLANT
SWISS CHARD Cool-season crop **Outdoors:** good **Indoors:** good **How to start:** seed	**Minimum container size for 1 plant:** 12 inches wide, 8 inches deep **Container Varieties:** Lucullus, Fordhook Giant, Burpee's Rhubarb Chard	**Approximate yield per plant:** ½-1 pound **Eventual spacing:** 8 inches	**Depth to plant seed:** ½ inch	**Days to mature vegetables:** 60

photo: Burpee See

CULTURE AND HARVESTING

Culture

No other vegetable can match Swiss Chard for producing so much edible vegetable in such a small area. It is virtually pest-free, and will withstand the heat of the summer which forces lettuce and spinach to go to seed. It can be planted any time of year indoors.

Swiss Chard is actually a beet that produces leaves like spinach and stalks like asparagus. Sow seeds 1 inch apart, later thinning to 8 inches.

Harvesting

Pull off the outer leaves as needed and before the stalks become stringy. If planted in the spring, the first leaves should be mature in 60 days. Following a summer planting, leaves are ready in 45 days.

PLANT	CONTAINER	YIELD	DEPTH TO PLANT SEED	DAYS TO MATURE PLANT
TOMATO Warm-season crop **Outdoors:** excellent **Indoors:** excellent **How to start:** seed or transplants	**Minimum container size for one plant:** full-sized plants: 2 gallons of soil or a 12-18 inch diameter tub compact plants: 6-inch flowerpot **Container Varieties:** Patio, Pixie, Tumblin' Tom, Small Fry VFN, Better Boy VFN, Early Girl, Salad Top, Super Fantastic VFN, Sunripe VFN, Toy Boy, Tiny Tim	**Approximate yield per plant:** 30-100 cherry tomatoes or 15 full-sized tomatoes **Eventual spacing:** 12 inches	**Depth to plant seed:** ½ inch	**Days to mature vegetables:** 50-7

No training—spra

Single stem staking

Multiple stem stak

Culture

Isn't it nice everyone's favorite vegetable is easy to grow and ideally suited for outdoor or indoor container gardening?

Any standard variety of tomato can be grown in a container holding five gallons of soil per plant. Those varieties which have been developed especially for container gardening are adapted to extremely small spaces—the tiniest can produce cherry tomatoes in a 4-inch flower pot!

Seeds can be started indoors. For fast germination, start plants in peat pots and keep the soil warm. After the seeds emerge from the soil, keep in sunlight 12 hours a day in peat pots. If they are started more than 3 or 4 weeks before transplanting, plant growth will shift into neutral. Either transplant into a larger pot indoors, or just wait until outside air temperature stays above 60° regularly. If you use nursery seedlings, bury ½ to ¾ of the stem and root ball.

Tomato stems are unique because they can sprout roots when buried, thus hurrying along the growth of the plant. If the stem is longer than 6 inches, tilt the root ball horizontally so it won't be buried more than 3 inches below the surface. Don't try to bend the leafy part of the stem so it protrudes straight from the ground. It will straighten by itself in a day or two.

There has always been controversy on pinching tomato plants to one stem versus letting them sprawl. Training the single stem plants on a stake and pinching out the side shoots gives you larger fruits a little earlier. Letting the stems divide and multiply will give you small fruits, but there will be more of them. More foliage will give better protection from sun scald. Take your pick, either system will give you delicious vine-ripened tomatoes.

A cage, tower, trellis or stake should be used with either a one or multiple stem system to keep tomatoes off the ground, away from pests and diseases. Use a figure-8 tie to fasten cloth strips or twist-ems between the stems and the structure.

Be sure to water plants regularly and feed weekly with a vegetable plant food. If the plants are being over-watered or over-fertilized, the plants will not blossom, or else existing blossoms will drop. To correct this, pinch out the top of the growing shoot, and reduce the water given the plant (but not to the point of wilting).

The tomato pollinates within a very narrow temperature range. If the night air is warmer than 75° F, or a prolonged rainy condition lasts for several days, fruit will not develop. The tomato flower contains both male and female parts, so the pollen stays with the same flower and does not have to be transferred to another flower. Pollen is produced most abundantly on sunny days between 10:00 a.m. and 4:00 p.m. To increase fruit set, shake the plants between these times, or tap with a pencil. Indoors there are no winds or bees to move those pollen grains. For earlier tomatoes, spray a fruit-setting hormone to encourage fruit pollination.

Tomatoes are very sensitive to changes in moisture while fruit is developing. A dry spell can cause the tomatoes to crack or split. Irregular watering will cause the bottom of the tomato to become leathery and brown, called blossom end rot.

The hairs and bumps on the sides of the stems are perfectly normal and not "warts." They are little pockets of oil, which when broken give off the aromatic tomato smell. If these blisters of oil appear on the faces of teenagers they are not accepted so well!

Harvesting

Tomatoes ripen from the inside out, so even when the outside skin is green, the flesh may already be ripe. It is best to pick them when they have reached their full color. If tomatoes are picked green, place them in a paper bag to trap the ethylene gas they are producing and speed maturity and color changes.

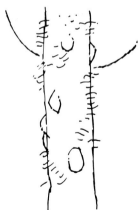

A normal stem with hairs and oil glands.

HERBS

Herbs are small indispensable plants that have oils locked in small glands in their leaves, seeds or fruits. As a group, they also share the need to be reached by sunlight for at least half a day, preferably without any shading.

Start from seed, or transplant herbs from nursery seedlings. Several herbs can be grown together or used in other vegetable or flower containers. The taller herbs generally need 8-10" between plants for their bushy, spreading growth. Be sure the plants do not become crowded or pot bound or the top growth will become weakened. Repot at least once a year or start another crop.

Water the containers well, then not again until the surface feels dry. Annual herbs should not be left outside in freezing weather. Perennial herbs, such as mint, chives, lavendar, thyme, woodruff, tarragon, winter savory and sage, can be sunk in sand or put in a cold frame or basement until spring.

Fresh leaves can be used any time. To dry herbs for winter use, place them on a cookie sheet in an electric oven. Turn on the lowest possible heat and leave the door ajar. In a gas stove the pilot light provides enough heat. Dry the herbs for 2-3 hours, place in a glass or metal container and seal tightly.

FLOWERS

Really all flowers can be grown adequately in containers. Annual varieties are best suited because of their constant prolific blooms, and because they need very little soil in which to flourish. A creative gardener can mix interesting color combinations of flowers, vegetables, herbs and even background curtains of climbing vines.

To keep flowers blooming continuously indoors or out, pick off faded blossoms and seed pods.

FRUIT

Not only strawberries, but other small fruits, citrus and even tree fruits, can be grown in containers no bigger than a half barrel.

STRAWBERRIES

Choose between everbearing varieties which fruit in the spring and fall, and June-bearing which produce berries the summer following planting. Space plants 10" apart, or insert in a strawberry jar, making sure the crown of the plant (the part of the stem where the leaves are attached) is even with the soil line. For everbearing varieties, pick off all the flowers until July. June-bearing varieties will blossom, but a crop will not be produced until the next summer. Strawberries can stand light frost but should be covered with a 3-4" layer of mulch and heavy plastic or a tarpaulin during the winter.

SMALL FRUITS

Although your harvest of raspberries, blackberries, blueberries, currants, gooseberries and grapes won't be abundant, these fruits are definite conversation pieces when growing in tubs.

You can recognize a raspberry, regardless of its color, by the hole in its core when it is picked. It is the hardiest cane fruit, and most

worthwhile after seeing the supermarket price for raspberries—fresh or frozen.

Blackberries have a solid core that stays with the fruit when it is picked. Of the two types, erect and trailing, only the trailing berries, or dewberry or loganberry as they are also called, need a support trellis.

There are two distinct types of grapes—American and European. The names do not distinguish their origin but where the bunches of fruit are borne on the vine. American varieties such as *Concord, Tokay,* and *Muscat* fruit on buds a long distance on the cane away from the vine. European varieties, with very European names, bear in clusters very close to the main stem. Training and pruning are dependent on which variety you are growing.

Blueberries are a good fruit to grow in containers since the soil can be mixed to provide the acidity blueberries so love. Use a mix of one part peat moss and one part loam. Set plants about 4 feet apart. Plant 1 per tub, which is at least the size of a pail.

Currants and gooseberries are fruits you can rarely buy in the store, but grow easily in containers for use in jellies, pies or fresh use.

For further information on the culture of each fruit, ask your county extension agent.

CITRUS FRUITS

Mandarin oranges, kumquats, lemons, limes and even pineapples can be grown indoors or out in containers. Citrus does not grow at temperatures below 55°, but thrives in a humid atmosphere between 70-90°.

It is possible to start trees from seeds contained in fruit purchased from the grocery store—although results are often disappointing. It is more successful to buy started plants.

Plant or transplant into a container with a soil mix of one part sand, one part peat, one part loam. Give the container a thorough soaking and allow to dry between waterings. In air-conditioned homes in the summer or heated homes in the winter, the trees will require more frequent watering. Fertilize sparingly but at least once a month.

Citrus trees appreciate being outside in mild weather. This ripens the wood and assures a fruit crop for the winter. Don't put the trees outdoors before the air temperature is close to what they had been accustomed to indoors. Be sure to bring indoors when temperatures regularly dip below 55°.

TREE FRUITS

With genetic and grafted dwarf fruit trees now available, you can have 4-foot trees bearing full-sized fruit in just 2 or 3 seasons after planting. Even tender plants can be grown outdoors and wheeled in for winter protection, or to shade if desert heat is your problem. Plant your trees in containers that are just 2 or 3 inches wider than the roots of the tree. For a bare-root tree, this will be about the size of a five-gallon can or a 12-inch diameter tub. Repot it the following

spring. If the dwarf is grafted, make sure the scar at the base of the trunk is always kept above the ground.

Use one part soil and one part peat moss for the soil mix. Every couple of months leach the soil of any salts by turning on a hose to allow enough water to run into the container, through the container's soil mixture, and out the bottom. Leave the water on for 20 minutes.

Containerized fruit trees need at least 6-8 hours of sunlight daily. Many varieties need to be thinned or they will overset fruit and the fruit can snap the branches.

Some fruits cannot set fruit by themselves. Some apples, pears, plums, almonds, and all sweet cherries need another variety close by

photo: Stark Bros. Nursery

to cross-pollinate. Trees of sour cherries, nectarines, apricots and peaches can be grown alone, but the other tree fruits will not bear unless another variety is growing nearby or grafted onto the tree.

Most fruit trees can be moved to a protected area during the winter, but need to be chilled and dormant for several months. Give the tree a good soaking after cold weather comes. Mulch the container with straw or newspapers and cover with a cardboard carton from a large appliance. The soil will still expand and contract despite the mulch, so use a plastic or wood tub (other than ceramic or clay) to prevent damage during the winter. Add no more water until spring.